PHILIP'S *Red Books* *showing the u*

LOCAL STREET ATLAS

GW00361030

SHREWSBURY
TELFORD

ALBRIGHTON · BRIDGNORTH · BROSELEY · CHURCH STRETTON
MINSTERLEY · MUCH WENLOCK · NEWPORT · PONTESBURY
SHAWBURY · SHIFNAL · WELLINGTON · WEM

CONTENTS

LEGEND

	Pedestrianized / Restricted Access
	Track
	Built Up Area
----	Footpath
	Stream
	River
Lock	Canal
■	Railway / Station
●	Post Office
P P+	Car Park / Park & Ride
C	Public Convenience
+	Place of Worship
→	One-way Street
i	Tourist Information Centre
8 8	Adjoining Pages
	Area Depicting Enlarged Centre
	Emergency Services
	Industrial Buildings
	Leisure Buildings
	Education Buildings
	Hotels etc.
	Retail Buildings
	General Buildings
	Woodland
	Orchard
	Recreational / Parkland
	Cemetery

www.philips-maps.co.uk

First published in 2006 by Estate Publications

This edition published by Philip's
a division of Octopus Publishing Group Ltd
www.octopusbooks.co.uk
Endeavour House, 189 Shaftesbury Avenue
London WC2H 8JY
An Hachette UK Company
www.hachette.co.uk

Fourth impression 2011
10/06-06

ISBN 978-0-540-09333-5

© Philip's 2008

Ordnance Survey®

This product includes mapping data licensed from
Ordnance Survey® with the permission of the Controller of
Her Majesty's Stationery Office. © Crown copyright 2006.
All rights reserved. Licence number 100011710.

No part of this publication may be reproduced, stored in
a retrieval system or transmitted in any form or by any
means, electronic, mechanical, photocopying, recording or
otherwise, without the permission of the Publishers and the
copyright owner.

Hindford · Welsh Frankton · Lee · Colemere · Wolverley · Paddolgreen · Edstaston · Prees Green · Hawk Lake · Marc
B5009 · B5068 · A495 · Lower Frankton · A528 · Hordley · B5063 · B5065 · A49 · Weston
Whittington · Babbinswood · Kenwick · English Frankton · Newtown · Wem · 19 · Aston
stry · Middleton · Lower Hordley · Cockshutt · Brownheath · Noneley · Loppington · B5063 · Lee Brockhurst · Boo
Millenio · S · Rednal · Bagley · Petton · Burlton · SLEAP AIRFIELD · Preston Brockhurst · Stanton on Hine Heat
A5 · Morda · Ball · Haughton · Weston common · Weston Lullingfields · Alderton · Clive · Preston Gubbals · Moreton Corbet
West Felton · Wykey · Marton · Myddle · Yorton · Grinshill · Shawbury · 16 · Much
A483 · Maesbury · Maesbury Marsh · Morton · Eardiston · B4397 · A5 · Stanwardine in the Fields · Harmer Hill · Hadnall · Astley · Gr Wyt
Waer · Llynclys · Woolston · Ruyton-XI-Towns · Brownhill · 18 · Baschurch · Merrington · Bomere Heath · 18 · Poynton Green · Wa
Knockin · Kinnerley · Hopton · Little Ness · B5067 · Yeaton · Albrighton · Bings Heath · Roden
Four Crosses · Crickheath · Maesbrook · Dovaston · Nesscliffe · Wilcott · Great Ness · Leaton · Fitz · A5124 · Harlescott · 7 · Haughton · Roden
Domgay · Crosslanes · Pentre · Felton Butler · Ensdon · A5 · Montford Bridge · R. Severn · B5067 · 6 · Mount Pleasant · B5062 · Ro
Llandrinio · Melverley · Shrawardine · Montford · Bicton · 17 · Monkmoor · Uffington · Withington
Criggion · Coedway · Alberbury · Ford · 17 · Gains Park · 10 · 11 · Upton Magna · A5
Crewgreen · Rowton Castle · Shoot Hill · 8 · 9 · Copthorne · Shrewsbury · Emstrey · Norton
Middletown · Wollaston · Rowton · Cardeston · Nox · Hanwood · A488 · A5 · Meole Brace · 15 · Atcham · Wroxeter
Garma Bank · Halfway House · Stretton Heath · Yockleton · 16 · 12 · 13 · S · 14 · Betton Pool · Cross Houses · Berrington · Donni
458 · Westbury · Stoney Stretton · Edge · Lea · Bayston Hill · Bomere Pool · A458 · C
Vennington · Farley · Hinton · Plealey · Great Lyth · A49 · Condover · Cantlop · Cound Brook · Cound
Aston Rogers · Westley · Asterley · Longden · Oaks · Stapleton · Pitchford · Golding · Cress
Rowley · Minsterley · 20 · Pontesbury · Longden Common · Acton Burnell · Acton Pigott
Brockton · Binweston · Worthen · Leigh · Ploxgreen · Habberley · Church Pulverbatch · Dorrington · Frodesley · Ruckley · Kenley
Marton · Betton · Hope · Pulverbatch · Longnor · Church Preen · Stre Westu
Meadowtown · Snailbeach · 502 · Stiperstones · Picklescott · Woolstaston · Leebotwood · Hughley
Wotherton · Black Marsh · Gravels · Pennerley · Shelve · The Bog · Bridges · Ratlinghope · All Stretton · Enchmarsh · Plaish · Bo
bury · Priest Weston · The Marsh · Corndon Hill 504 · Linley Hill 411 · 516 · 50 · Cardington · Gretton · Longville in the Dale · Eastho
Hyssington · Linley · Norbury · Church Stretton · 459 · Hope Bowdler · East Wall · Rushbury · Shiptor
B4386 · Snead · Lydham · More · Asterton · Little Stretton · 51 · Minton · Wall under Heywood · Ticklerton · Edge · Broadstone · Sta
Lea · Myndtown · Marshbrook · Hatton · Acton Scott · Eaton under · Holdgate

SHROPSHIRE

Ternhill
Sutton
Chipnall
Croxton
Slindon
Yarnfield
STAFFORD
By-Sto

Woodseaves
Cheswardine
Sugnall
Sturbridge
Norton Bridge
Shallowford
Chebsey

Rosehill
Stoke Heath
Wollerton
Wistanswick
Bishop's Offley
Adbaston
High Offley
Wootton
Great Bridgeford
Whitg

Hodnet **54**
Stoke on Tern
Lockleywood
Knighton
Shebdon
Woodseaves
Ellenhall
Lawnhead
A5013

Eccleshall
R. Sow
A519

53
Peplow
Hinstock
Ellerton
Weston Jones
Norbury
Ranton
Seighford
Coton Clanford

High Hatton
Childs Ercall
Sambrook
Long Compton
Derrington
M6
Do

Ellerdine Heath
Eaton upon Tern
Howle
Puleston
Sutton
Gnosall
Haughton
A518
Coppenhal

Gold Hatton Heath
Great Bolas
Tibberton
B5062
Edgmond Marsh
A41
Ferton
Aqualate Mere
Gnosall Heath
Allimore Green

Rowton
Cherrington
Adeney
Edgmond
22
23
Newport
Chetwynd Aston
Moreton
Church Eaton
Bradley
Lev

Waters Upton
Brugington
Outwoods
High Onn
Mitton
Penk

ELFORD & WREKIN
Kynnersley
Sleapford
A442
21
Lilleshall
Great Chatwell
Orslow
Brineton
Marston
Shropshire Union Canal
Whiston

ongdon on Tern
B5063
Hortonwood
Muxton
Heath Hill
Weston Heath
Blymhill
Wheaton Aston
Lapley
Stretton

24
Shawbirch
25
26
27
28
29
Donnington
Sheriffhales
Weston-under-Lizard
Watling A5
Street
S

Admaston
Leegomery
A442
Marsh
reen
Wrockwardine
Hadley
Redhill
Cracklebank
Bishop's Wood
Belvide Resr
Horsebrook

B50
30
31
32
33
34
35
A5
A5379
B4379
Kiddemore Green
Brewoo

Wellington
Ketley
Oakengates
St Georges
A41
Coven

gton
Aston
7
Lawley
Stafford Park
S
47
M54
Codsall Wood
M54

hton
The Wrekin 407
Little Wenlock
36
37
38
A64
39
Shifnal
Tong
48
49
Albrighton
3
Codsall
Oaken
La Foodhou
Green
ngwood

Dawley
Telford
Strichley
Halesfield
Kemberton
A464
Bilbrook

Leighton
40
41
42
43
Ryton
A41
Wergs
Oxl

Buildwas
Coalbrookdale
Woodside
Madeley
Brockton
Grindle
Boningale
Beckbury
Tettenhall
Wolverhampton

Sheinton
A4169
Ironbridge
44
45
46
Coalport
R. Worfe
Burnhill Green
The Great Pool
Perton
A41

Homer
Broseley
Norton
Badger
Ackleton
Pattingham
Trescott
A449
Sec

Wyke
Barrow
B4376
Stockton
Shipley
A454
Lower Penn
A463

Much Wenlock
54
Willey
R. Severn
Worfield
Hilton
Upper Ludstone
Seisdon
Trysull
Wombourne

ope
The Smithies
Nordley
Ashley Abbots
Rudge Heath
Staffordshire & Worcestershire Canal
Himley

Acton Round
Haughton
Rindleford
Bobbington
Halfpenny Green
Swindon

Aston Eyre
A458
Morville
Bridgnorth
Roughton
Claverley
Upper Aston
Heathton
The

Monkhopton
B4368
Upton Cresset
52
53
Village
A4179

Weston
Chetton
Eardington
Quatford
WOLVERHAMPTON BUSINESS

Middleton Priors

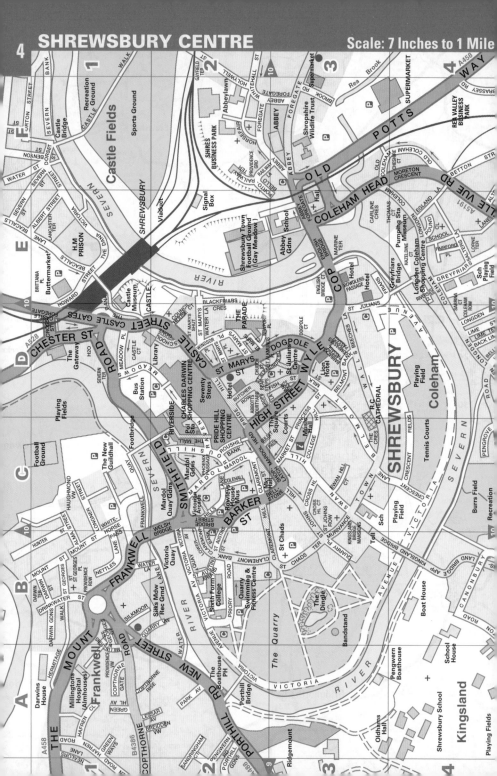

E   **F**   **G**   **H**

Shrewsbury 1403

Travelodge

Livestock Market

BATTLEFIELD RD

BOWMEN WAY

A49

ROBERT JONES WAY

P H

A53

Albrightlee House

1

P

Enterprise Roundabout

LINK ROAD

A5112

ROAD

Battlefield Roundabout

BATTLEFIELD ROAD

SHREWSBURY ROAD

Battlefield

Kendricks Rough

Pool Rough

GUARD WAY

Works

S BATTLEFIELD

Lion Coppice

The Bern

Albrightlee

Sunderton Pool

2

Dell Farm

ARLINGTON

SUNDORNE RETAIL PARK

HOVE END

HALLAM DR

HALLAM

GREATFORD

DAWSON

DRIVE

LANE

PEACEHAVEN

Harlescott

P+

ARLINGTON

GOWAN

FARRAN GRO

GREATFORD GRN

Depot

Superstore

WAY

HENLEY WY

HALLAM

Sundorne Farm

3

LESCOTT

Bowling Alley

LESCOTT LANE INDUSTRIAL ESTATE

Works

KENDAL

NORTH

ROAD

BATTLEFIELD ROAD

FEATHERBED

Harlescott

Works

SWALLOW

RAMSEY MEWS

KESTREL

HECKER

PACK

HERON

SWIFT

PARTRIDGE CL

CURLEW

Sundorne Castle Farm

4

AMBLESIDE

ORION PARK

KENDAL

ROAD

MEADOW

HAWKSTONE RD

COUNTDON DR

HARLESCOTT

Liby

CORN DON DR

STANTON

MOSTON GRN

School

LANE FEATHERBED

CRESCENT

ARLINGTON

CRESCENT

AYLEBURY

LINNET

THE SPRINGS

WREN CL

THE BRAIDS

KEYS

KESTREL CL

GOLDCREST DR

DRIVE

LARK CL

CURLEW CL

AYLEBURY

KINGFISHER

WOOD

SHREWSBURY BY-PASS

HITCHURCH

ROSEWAY

BISBREE

BAUGHMOND

CORNDON

Schools

CRESCENT

BROUGHTON ROAD

DRIVE

MOSTON

FARM FIELD

Liby

Recreation Ground

CRAIG

ALLERTON

CLAVERLEY ROAD

CLAVERLEY CRES

QUATFORD

NORTHSIDE DR

DRIVE

W HITINGTON

HOLGATE

THE HASSOCKS

AYLEBURY

5

ALBERT

ROSEDALE

SUNDORNE CRESCENT

SUNDORNE AVENUE

CORNDON CRES

EAST CRES

CORNDON RD

EBURY

MEADOW

FERNDALE DR

AVENUE

ALLERTON ROAD

ALLERTON ROAD

ROAD

Sports Ground

SUNDORNE

Squash Centre

Harlescott Youth Centre

Sundorne Pool

B5062

WELLINGTON CL

GOMERY

MARLBOROUGH

Pimley Roughs

Recreation Ground

Welti Tennis & Leisure Centre

The Gables Farm

6

Golf Driving Range

RIVER SEVERN

Shropshire Way

Pimley Bridge

Pimley Manor

SHREWSBURY BY-PASS

A49

Underdale Hall

E   **F**   11   **G**   S   **H**

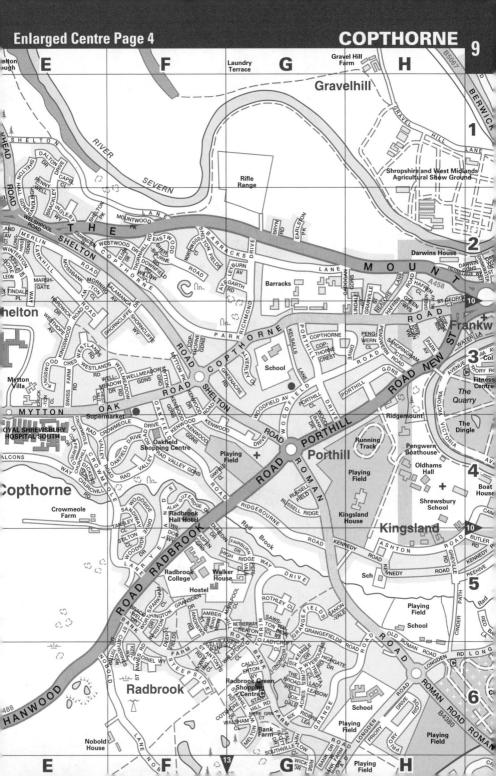

Golf Driving Range

Underdale Hall Farm

Schools

Monkmoor Farm

Monkmoor

Manor

ROAD

SEVERN

A49

BY - PASS SHREWSBURY

Uffington

Manor Farm

Works

MONKMOOR IND EST

Works

Sewage Works

Police H.Q

Crowmere House

Bridge Farm

Severn Way

RIVER

SEVERN

School

School

Playing Field

School

School

CARMEN

School

THE ELMS

Weir Hill Farm

Ferry House

BY - PASS

A5

Preston Farm

Preston

School

Playing Field

School

Robertsford

Weir

Ford Hill

SHREWSBURY

BY - PASS

A5

Playing Field

Sports Hall

Running Track

Shrewsbury College of Arts & Technology

Crematorium

Quarry Wood

A5064

A458

ROAD

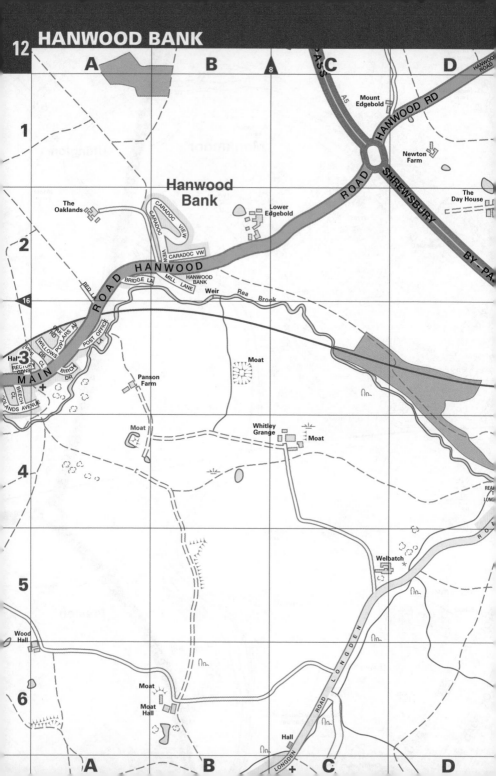

A   B   8   C   D

1

Hanwood Bank

Mount Edgebold

The Oaklands

CARADOC VIEW

CARADOC VIEW

Lower Edgebold

HANWOOD RD

Newton Farm

The Day House

2

CARADOC VW

HANWOOD

ROAD

SHREWSBURY

BY-PA

BRIDGE LA

MILL LANE

HANWOOD BANK

Weir

Rea Brook

RED LA

16

ROAD

POST OFFICE LA

OAK DR

POPLARS AV

Moat

WILLOWS

VINE DR

BIRCH DR

3

Hall

RECTORY GDNS

MAIN

Panson Farm

BEECH CL

DLANDS AVENUE

Moat

Whitley Grange

Moat

4

REA T LONG

Welbatch

5

Wood Hall

LONGDEN

ROAD

Moat

6

Moat Hall

Hall

LONGDEN

A   B   C   D

E F G H

Nobold House

Playing Field

9

Bank Farm

MELTON

SOUTH

ALDWICK DR

LOW

BANK DR

BANK FARM ROAD

RISE

HIGH

ROAD

LONG

PRIOR

Playing Field

ROAD

ROMAN RD

MOUSECROFT

LANE NOBOLD

NUFFIELD HOSPITAL

Playing Field

Sports Centre

School

LANE

STANLEY

MEOLE WK

MEOLE WK

MEOLE

SIMON CH

Hall

1

P

SILVER BIRCH DR

STATION ROAD

VICTORIA RD

ALEXANDRA

AVENUE

VICARAGE

CHURCH ROAD

Sch

Hall

Warehouses

FAIRLAWN

GDNS

Schools

BURNSIDE

GDNS

MAES

Depot

Nobold

GROVE

MERCIAN CL

SPETTLANE

LONGDEN

ROAD

WFAIRLAWN AV

LONSDALE

RIVING- TGN AV

FIELD

HOUSE

DRIVE

CHURCH ROAD

Nobold Hall Farm

Meole Village

ADSWOOD

ELSTREE

CRO... CRO...

WASHFORD

SINGLETON AV

ELS- WICK CL

CARNFORTH CL

MARY WEBB ROAD

NETLEY RD

SHOMERE

WASHFORD

ROAD

PEND...

MILNTHORPE CL

CHATFORD

DEPLEY CRES

14

2

HREWSBURY

LANE

PULLEY

A5

3

Rea Brook

LONGDEN

Redhill

ROAD

BY - PASS

PULLEY

PULLEY

LANE

LOWER

Travel Lodge

SHREWS SERVI

Garden Centre

i

Hanley House

Hook-a-gate

ducation Centre

GORSE

PARRYS

HANLEY

SIDE

POOL

OAK TREE

LANE

PARRS

LANE

LANE

LANERDALE

PULLEY

LANE

GREEN

HOLLIES

HOLLIES DR

Pulley

Pulley Farm

Pulley Hall

LANE

PULLEY

LANE

4

LANSDOWNE

BOURNE

RISE

LANSDOWNE

DR

CRESCENT

Bayston Hill

14

HEA

Spring

FAIRVIEW DR

MAYFIE...

LANGFORD

FAIRVIEW DR

SUNFIELD GDNS

MAYFIELD

GRO

BERWYN DR

LONG

HOLLAND CL

WENT- WORTH CL

Hall

Playground

Sch

Sch

CASTLE LA

DRIVE

CASTLE RD

BROAD

OAK CRES

BUTCHER

CHESTNUT DR

LODGE

CROSS RDS

CRO...

THE COMMON

The

BURNE VW

ROAD

ROAD

HEREFORD

A49

5

6

ROOKFIELD

BR

BREDDEN WY

LYTHWOOD

ROAD

GED...

LYTHWOOD

MEADOW

ROAD

Shopping Centre

DAVINA GDNS

CHRISTCHURCH

BEECHES DR

Liby

POPLAR CRESC

MALL...

CLARKEFIELDS

ROAD

R

Sch

Lythwood Hall

Stanley Parker Playing Field

Community Centre

BEECHES

TWO ASHES

BEECHES

MEADOW BROOK

GLEBE

YEW TREE

BURNELL CL

GLEBE

LANGLEY

Football Ground

Hall

NEW- BROOK

WELLBURY

SPRINGMERE

CORNWALL DRIVE

BANK

CARADOC VW

KENDRICKS

BURG

Lythwood Farm

GROVE

EDGE CL

ERIC LOCK RD

ERIC LOCK

NEW-

BETLEY

LANE

BETLEY TER

Lythwood House

AMBLECO

BEDDOES

White House

E F G H

Cemetery

Rec Grnd

Kempsfield Hostel

Shrewsbury Municipal Golf Course

HEREFORD ROAD

HAZELDINE ROAD

Golf Course

Club House

OTELEY ROAD

Sutton Grange

Weir

Sutton

Meole Brace

MEOLE BRACE RETAIL PARK

The New Meadow Shrewsbury Town F.C. (Under Construction)

Percy Throwers Garden Centre

ROAD OTELEY

Superstore

Mary Webb Road

SHREWSBURY ROAD

A5

Travel Lodge

SHREWSBURY SERVICES

Garden Centre

Stone Quarry

Sharpestone Hill

Betton Alkmere

HEREFORD ROAD

Sharpstones Lane

Moat

CROSS LANE

The Common

The Burgs Fort

Bomere Farm

Bomere Pool

E   F   11   G   A5   H

Crematorium

Quarry Wood

Longner Hall

Cricket Ground

Ravens Nest

1

New College RD

HUXLE

WOOLEA

CHILD
RENS
WY

Schs

Football Grnd

SPRING
FIELD

RIPPLE
CL

KNIGHTSBRIDGE

SOUTHGATE
DR

SALTNEY
CL

SALT-
DEAN
DR

HOL-
BORN
DRIVE AV

DR'N

HIGHBURY
CL

SALCO

LEXINGTON

KINGSTON

Emstrey Rough

A5064

BY - PASS

ROAD

Emstrey Island

RIVER

SEVERN

Emstrey

Mere Pool

SHREWSBURY
BUSINESS
PARK

LANE

Garden Centre

EMSTREY

2

BROADWAY

Recreation Ground

THIEVES

EMSTREY

B4380

BANK

ROAD

BY - PASS   SHREWSBURY

Weeping Cross Island

WENLOCK

3

Boreton Grange

WENLOCK

Betton Strange Hall

Bettonfield

Betton Strange

Fox Farm

Chilton Larches

4

Betton Grange

Chilton Grove

5

Betton Coppice

ROAD

A458

6

Pit (dis)

Lower Betton

E   F   G   H

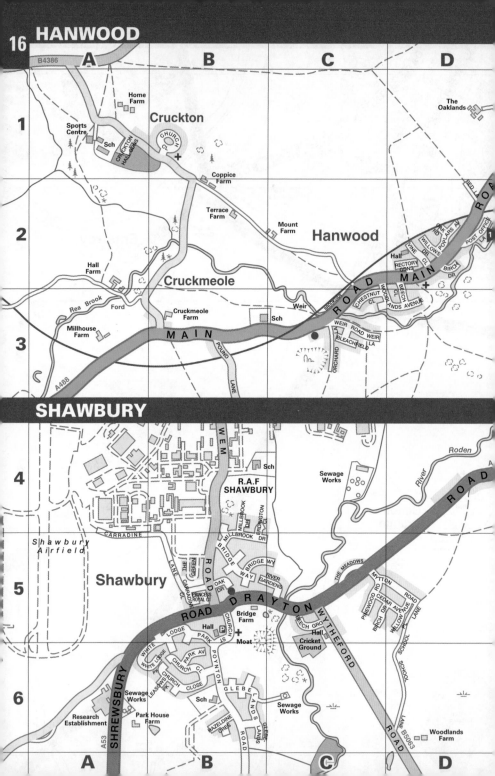

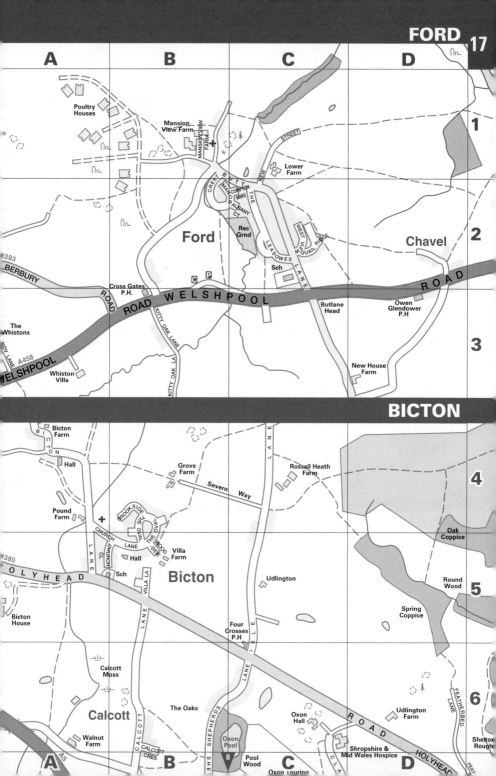

A B C D

Poultry Houses

Mansion View Farm

MANSION VIEW FARM

COMPTON MWS

MANOR ALBANY CT

CREST

BUTT

THE

NEW STREET

Lower Farm

Ford

Rec Grnd

WEST VW

QUAIL RIDGE

LEASOWES LANE

Sch

Chavel

1

2

A3393

BERBURY

ROAD

ROAD

WELSHPOOL

Cross Gates P.H.

KITTY OAK LANE

KITTY OAK LA

ROAD

Butlane Head

Owen Glendower P.H

The Whistons

A458

WELSHPOOL

INDY LANE

Whiston Villa

New House Farm

3

Bicton Farm

BICTON

Hall

Grove Farm

LANE

Rossall Heath Farm

Severn Way

4

Oak Coppice

Pound Farm

BROOK SIDE

THE OVAL

THE WOOD

CHURCH LANE

CHURCH CL

Hall

Sch

VILLA LA

Villa Farm

Bicton

Udlington

Round Wood

5

A380

HOLYHEAD

Bicton House

Spring Coppice

Four Crosses P.H

SLE LANE

Calcott Moss

SHEPHERDS LANE

FEATHERBED LANE

6

Calcott

The Oaks

Udlington Farm

CALCOTT

CALCOTT CRES

Oxon Hall

ROAD

HOLYHEAD

CLA

Walnut Farm

Oxon Pool

Pool Wood

Shropshire & Mid Wales Hospice

Shelto Rough

FEAT

A5

A

B

Oxon Louring

C

D

8

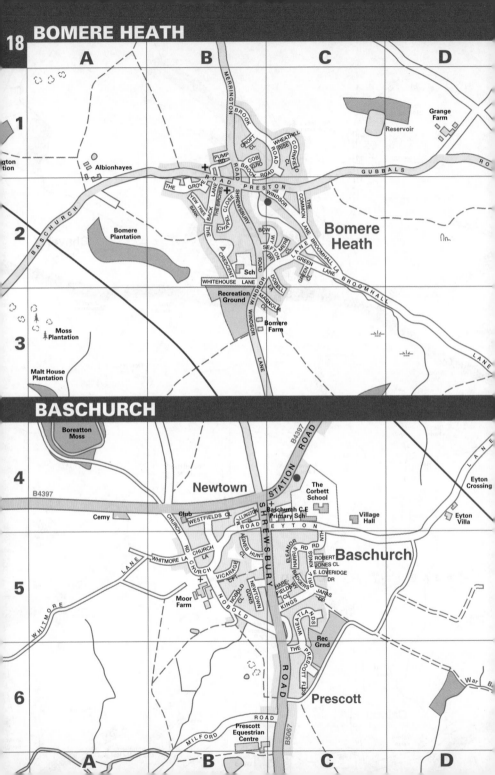

A B C D

1

Grange
Farm

Reservoir

Albionhayes

PUMP
RD

CROFT
COB
BROOK
GRO
WHEATHILL
RISE
CORNFIELD
CL
WINDSOR

BROOK ROAD

MERRINGTON

BROOK

ROAD

SHREWSBURY ROAD

PRESTON

GUBBALS

RO

THE GROVE
YEW TREE
BANK
THE BIRCHES
THE BIRCHES
CHAPEL CLOSE

THE COMMON LANE

2

Bomere
Plantation

Bomere
Heath

CRESCENT

BOW
WY
SEF
ION
MERE
CL

SEF
ION

SCH

WHITEHOUSE LANE

NOBELL

GREEN
GREEN
CL

BROOMHALL LA

LANE BROOMHALL

Recreation
Ground

WINDSOR
LA
MAGNOLIA
CL

WINDSOR ROAD

3

Moss
Plantation

Malt House
Plantation

Bomere
Farm

WINDSOR LANE

LANE

Boreatton
Moss

B4397

STATION ROAD

B4397 ROAD

LANE

4

Newtown

The
Corbett
School

Eyton
Crossing

Cemy

Club
WESTFIELDS CL

SHREWSBURY

Baschurch C E
Primary Sch

EYTON

Village
Hall

Eyton
Villa

WHITMORE LA

CHURCH RD

CHURCH LA

AGNES HUNT CL

ELLINGTON
ROAD

ELEANOR RD
HARRIS RD
KINKIN RD
ROBERT
JONES CL
E LOVERIDGE
DR

Baschurch

5

WHITMORE LANE

CHURCH

VICARAGE

NOBOLD

NOBOLD GDNS

NEWTOWN

HARE
FIELDS
CL
BLOOKERS
TRI

KINGS

JARAS
DR

Moor
Farm

WHEATLANDS
Rec
Grnd

6

THE PRESCOTT FLDS

Prescott

MILFORD ROAD

ROAD

B5067

War
B

Prescott
Equestrian
Centre

A B C D

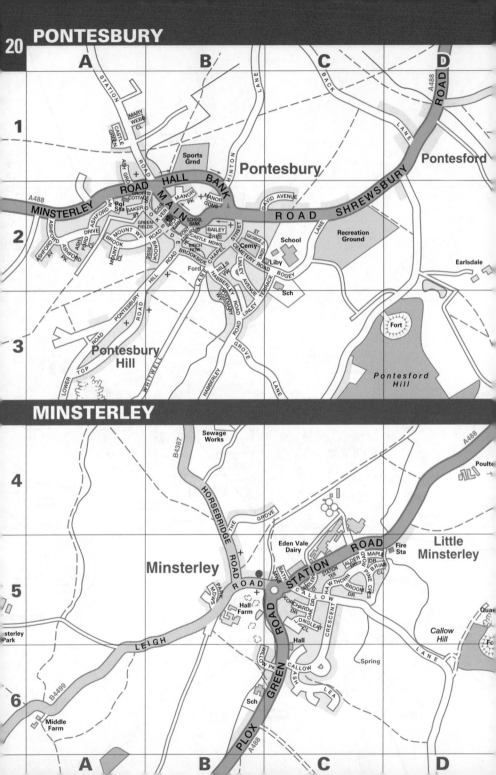

PONTESBURY

A **B** **C** **D**

STATION ROAD

MARY WEBB CL

CASTLE GREEN

1

Sports Grnd

HINTON LANE

LANE

Pontesbury

BACK LANE

A488 ROAD

Pontesford

ASH GRO

CROFTS COTTAGE

ROAD HALL BANK

A488

MINSTERLEY

Pol Sta

BAKER ST

GREEN FIELDS

MANOR PK

MANOR GDNS

DAVID AVENUE

ROAD SHREWSBURY

2

ASHFORD

ASHFORD DRIVE

ASHFORD CL

MOUNT WY

BROOK

MOUNT CL

BROOK RISE

BROOK HILL

ROAD MAIN

BRICK ST

CASTLE MDWS

SCHOOL BANK

BIRCH ROW

BROOKSIDE CHAPEL

BAILEY CRES

LINLEY AVENUE

NILLS

ST GEORGE'S

STREET

CEMETERY ROAD

Cemy

Liby

Sch

ST SNBD

SCH

TERRACE

School

BOGEY

Recreation Ground

ASHFORD RD

ASHFORD AV

ASHFORD PK

Ford

LANE

HABBERLEY

ROSEMARY

ROAD

Earlsdale

3

WHITWELL

LOWER TOP

ROAD PONTESBURY

ROAD

Pontesbury Hill

HABBERLEY ROAD

GROVE LANE

UNLEY AVENUE

Fort

Pontesford Hill

MINSTERLEY

A **B** **C** **D**

Sewage Works

B4387

HORSEBRIDGE ROAD

THE GROVE

A488

4

Poulte

Minsterley

PARK MDWS

ROAD

Hall Farm

Eden Vale Dairy

BATH MWB

STATION ROAD

SAMPLER

CALLOW

ORCHARD DR

STATION TER

HAWTHORN

ALDER DR

GROVE DR

MAPLE DR

PINE CRES

BRIAR CL

BROOM DR

Fire Sta

Little Minsterley

5

sterley Park

LEIGH

ROAD

GREEN ROAD

Hall

ORCHARD DR

LONGLEAT CL

CRESCENT

CALLOW

ASH LEA

Spring

LANE

Callow Hill

Quar

Fo

6

B4499

Middle Farm

PLOX A488

Sch

LOW PK

CALLOW

A **B** **C** **D**

A   B   C   D

1
B5062
New Inn Farm
SHREWSBURY ROAD
LONGWITHY LANE
CHETWYND ROAD
Newport Showground

WOODRIDGE CL
MENTONE CRES
SHREWSBURY ROAD
CHETWYND ROAD

2
FLATT RD
STACKYARD
HILLSIDE
Flatt Pit Farm
Sch
STREET LANE
NEWPORT RD
NEWPORT LANE
ROAD

KILVERT CL
ST PETERS WY
ROCK LA
PIPERS LANE
TURNERS LA
MANOR RD
SCHOOL RD
CONNERS
BAYLEY HILLS
ROBIN
Tickethouse Lock
Windy Meadows Farm
Rec Grnd

3
Sports Grnd
HIGH
Edgmond
Sewage Works
Edgmond Hall Residential Centre

4
Bridge Farm
Vauxhall House Farm
ROAD
MOORE

Church (rems of)
5
Brook Cottage
Longford
LONGFORD
Longford Hall
Pool Covert

Longford Mill Farm

6
Mill Wood
Watkins Covert
Aston Hill Covert
Aston   Hill

A   B   C   D

A B C D

1

B5063

Aqueduct

Mill House

MILLERS ROW

Longdon Hall

Redhouse Farm

Longdon on Tern

The Old Manor

Longdon House

LANE

2

Lower Farm

Lower Farm Cottages

Bratton Cottage

River Tern

3

Sand Pit

Bratton Hall Farm

RUSHMOOR

Lawn Farm

Bratton

Cheshire Coppice

Isombridge Farm

CHESHIRE

Moor Farm

Rushmoor

4

Sewage Works

5

Footbridge

Cheshire Coppice Cottages

COPPICE LANE

Allscott House

6 **Allscott**

Admaston

LITTLE MDW TO MEADOW DALE DR

PETERSDALE WK

B4394

A B 30 C D

STATION

BROOMF RD

E   **F**   **G**   **H**

The Moorings
Caravan Park
(dis) & Mobile Homes

Long Lane

The Farm

Long Lane
Farm

1

Eyton Moor

New Rookery

Eyton Lower
Lock
(dis)

Shropshire Union Canal (disused)

Weir

Weir

Eyton Lock
(disused)

2

Eyton House

26

Eyton upon the
Weald Moors

3 .on

Wheelwright
Covert

Bratton
Farm

Longpit
Coppice

Eyton Farm

4

HOPKINS HTH
HARRINGTON HEATH
SHERWOOD
ARROW RD
GUIS-BOURNE AV
FOREST CL
SPAN MDW

SPINNERS CT
WOODFORD
GLOVERS WY
GREENWOOD DR
SQUIRREL
CALLERTONS
SPAFIELD CL
RUITH FLD
RED WOOD
GLOVERS WY
DILWICH
GRANGE
SILKIN
GLADE
BUTTS
BROOK MDW
MDW
OAKFIELD
LEESES
CL
LOWRY CL
FOXS
FALLOW RD
RD
WHITEWAY DR
HOLT COPPICE
CLOSE
School
CROWDALE
MDW
NEWILL GRO
BRANDON
CONSTABLE DR
GAINSBOROUGH
REMBRANDT DR
GILES
MONET
TURNER CL
AV
COTE RD
STILE RISE
26

Shawbirch

A442

QUEENSWAY

5

DAVENPORT DR
SHAWBIRCH
ROAD
ROAD
ACORN WY
ACORN MWS
SWAN GATE
QUAIL GATE
LINNET GATE
TEE LAKE BOULEVARD
MERE GRO
ASPEN WAY
HORSE CHESTNUT WAY
GLADE WAY
GOSLING
PK
MARKS
McCORMICK DRIVE
Comm
Centre

SHAWBIRCH
ROUNDABOUT

Factory

Motel

WHITCHURCH DRIVE

ALDER MEAD CL
BRATTON CL
ELMSDALE CL
SHARP CL
BOSTOCK CL
BROCKWOOD CL
CORSE GLADE
BROCKWOOD GLADE
SPA CRES
ASTON SPA
SWIFT GATE
PLOVER CL
COPSE
MARSH CLOSE
MDW
LWR PARK MDW
COACH-MAN MDW
TEE LAKE
ST AGATHAS
HARLEY
ST PAULS
ST MARKS
ST BUSH CL
HITCOCKS CL
DASH CONEY
WOOD DR
FERNWOOD
UNDERTREES
GREENOAK DR
WHITCHURCH ROAD
APLEY CASTLE
APLEY
GATEHOUSE
A442

6

ROAD
STATION
SUTTON HILL
WELLINGTON RD
PEMBERTON WELL
THE BEECHES
BROOMFIELD
Comm
Centre

Playing
Field

Tee Lake

Dothill

Dothill
unty Schs

MORVILLE

EYTON VW
APLEY CT
SEVERN DRIVE
WHITCHURCH ROAD
LAWRENCE DR
ST PAULS
ST HELENS
EMPAL RISE
HAUGHMOND CT

THE (TELF

31

E   **F**   **G**   **H**

A B C D

1

Preston Moor

Crow Brook

Weir

Lo
ed

2

Wappenshall Moor

Mantle
Covert

25

Kinley
Farm

Wappenshall
Covert

Eyton Hall

3

Wappenshall

Wappenshall
Bridge

Hurley Brook

Park
Covert

Wappenshall
Farm

4

Wheatley
Grange

25

Shucks Lock
(dis)

A442

Apley Cottages

QUEENSWAY

QUEENSWAY

5

Apley Pool

GOSHAWK DR

SPARROWHAWK WY

PEREGRINE

Apley Cottages

GOLDCREST GRO

WOSPREY GRO

MANCHESTER

MONTGOMERY

LEEGOMERY
ROUNDABOUT

Leegomery

INDUSTRIAL
ESTATE

Pump
Wood

HADLEY

WOODPECKER DR

AVENUE

OKEHAMPTON DR

Lock
(dis)

SILKIN WAY

PORCHESTER

Shropshire Union Can (dissused)

Apley Castle
Park

PINTAIL DR

EIDER

MERLIN
COPPICE

DRIVE

CHICHESTER

BRANDON
RD

BARNES

BEAUFORT

SUNDERLAND
RD

AUSTER

WALLIS DR

BADER DR

CL

SPRUCE DR

BERBERIS
RD

MONARCH DR

HADLEY GDNS

PARK

HEDINGHAM
DR

CASTLE CROFT

DOVER RD

WARWICK WAY

ACRE RD

SANDAL CL

ASTLE

Apley Castle

GATEHOUSE GATEWAY
APLEY CASTLE

SHOVELLER DR

WIGEON
GRO

SHOVELLER
DR

MERGANSER

SHELLDUCK

ALBACORE
RD

BLENHEIM

SAXON CT

CACTUS DR

CLEMATIS RD

ANSON DR

ROAD

LONGTHOR
DR

6

IVE

A5223

THE PRINCESS ROYAL
(TELFORD DISTRICT GENERAL)
HOSPITAL

PASTEUR WAY

CURIE DR

NIGHTINGALE

TERESA

FLEMING WY

School

POOL FARM

CLOSE

LAWTON WY

AV

32
Comm

MEATLE

P

A B C D

E F G H

1

Lu

Sch

Preston Trust Homes

Preston upon the Weald Moors

Humber Brook

HUMBER LA
HUMBER EAST VIEW
HUM
HU

2

Hoo Farm Nature Park

P

Hoo

Hoo Hall

Crow Brook

Hoo Farm

Barracks

28

3

HORTON

Horton

Horton Farm

BASE ORDNANCE DEPOT

4

LANE

HORTON COURT

1-28

Hortonwood 50

28

5

CROWBROOK R/ABOUT

Hadley Park House Hotel

QUEENSWAY

LKIN

Nursery School

HADLEY PARK ROUNDABOUT

ORCHARD FARM R/ABOUT

HORTONWOOD

HORTON

HORTONWOOD

HORTONWOOD

35

30

31 32

33

37

RAILFREIGHT TERMINAL DEVELOPMENT

A518

QUEENSWAY

1

10

HORTONWOOD

7

NEW TRENCH RD

NEW

HORTONWOOD R/ABOUT

MOORE DRIVE

VIEWLANDS

OAKLANDS

STRA

6

Works

A442

2

HORTON LA

A518

NEW TRENCH ROAD

EDWARD TER

TRENCH

PRESTON GROVE

DAKWOOD DRI

ALBERT VILLAS

P

BROAD ROAD

TENBURY

CHURCH

AV

GORDON

WOODH

HORTON RD

BROADWAY

WOMBRIDGE

MILL

ASH

PINEWOOD

E F JUBILEE TER TRENCH RD **G** SFIELD **H** School

33

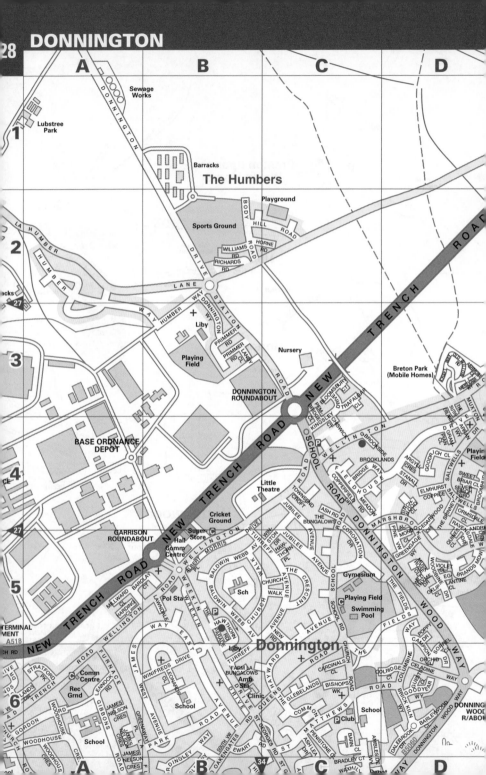

A B C D

1 Lubstree Park
Sewage Works

Barracks
The Humbers
Playground

BODY HILL ROAD
Sports Ground
HORNE RD
WILLIAMS RD
RICHARDS RD

LA HUMBER LA
2 HUMBER
HUMBER WAY
LANE
STATION ROAD
27

Liby
PRIMMER RD
PRIMMER RD
3 Playing Field
Nursery
DONNINGTON ROUNDABOUT
Breton Park (Mobile Homes)

BASE ORDNANCE DEPOT
NEW TRENCH ROAD
SCHOOL ROAD
BLOOMSBURY
PEMBRIDGE
KINGSLEY
CHISWICK RD
TRAFALGAR
BROOKSIDE
FIELDHOUSE
BRIDGE WAY
COPPERFIELD MEADOW
BROOKLANDS
ARGYLE CRES
STANALL DR
4 Little Theatre
TOWNSEND CROFT
ASH RD
CORONATION DR
MARSHBROOK
ELMHURST COPPICE
THE
Cricket Ground
JUBILEE
THE BUNGALOWS
WELLINGTON DRIVE
ALBERT MORRIS
TUIWINK
JUBILEE ST
DR
HAW-THORN PL
AVENUE
GREENGAGE

GARRISON ROUNDABOUT
Super-Store
Hall Comm Centre
BALDWIN WEBB AV
CHURCH AVENUE
THE CRESCENT
Gymasium
THE FIELDS
5 NEW TRENCH ROAD
MILLWARD CL
HARDING CL
BARCLAY CT
Pol Sta
WREKIN
BALDWIN WEBB AV
Sch
CHURCH WALK
NEW AVENUE
SCHOOL RD
Playing Field
Swimming Pool
FIELDS
27

TERMINAL MENT
A518
CH RD
NEW TRENCH ROAD
WELLINGTON ROAD
WAY
HAWTHORN PARADE
Liby
TURREFF
Donnington
ROAD
CHURCH ROAD
THE
WAY
POPPY

STRATFORD
Comm Centre
Rec Grnd
JAMES NELSON CRES
FURNACE
WEST
WINIFREDS DRIVE
JAMESWAY EAST
LEONARD RD
School
GREENWAY
ROAD
AVENUE
FARM LA BUNGALOWS
Amb Sta
Clinic
QUEENS
CARDINALS CL
GLEBELANDS
BISHOPS
MATTHEWS
ROAD
School
Club
DONNINGTON WOOD R/ABOU

6 WOODHOUSE CRE
School
JAMES NELSON CRES
RINGLEY
OAKENGATES
EWART
ST GEORGES RD
COMMON
BARN
PENISTONE CT
BRADLEY CT
B5060
DONNINGTON
WOODWAY
DALESBROOK

A B C D

E   F   G   H

21

KYNNERSLEY DRIVE

NEW TRENCH RD

WELLINGTON

A518

WELLINGTON RD

Monument

School

Lilleshall

1

Cricket Grnd

Youth Centre

HILLSIDE

HILLSIDE EAST

ROAD

LIMEKILN

LANE

WILLMOO   LANE

Old Farm La

Lilleshall Hall Farm

ST MICHAELS CL

ROCK ACRES

CHURCH MDW

CHURCH

Cemy

The Incline

2

Honnington

YEW TREE DR

School

Old Hall

Honnington Grange

ROAD

ABBEY

CHURCH

21

WELLINGTON

Lilleshall Grange

ROAD

ABBEY

3

The Oaks

Remains of Augustinian Abbey

NELSON WY

MERRINGTON RD

Grange Cottages

Sulphur Piece Plantation

MUXTON LANE

LANESIDE

GRANVILLE DR

THE PADDOCK

FOSTERLEY GRO

PERIVALE CL

CHALICE

MILLERS CROFT

JAMES CROFT

ABBEY

ROAD

LILYHURST RD

Abbey Farm

4

HOLLAND DR

MARSHBROOK

LYTHAM GRN

DRIVE

Muxton

Lilleshall Grove

5

Sch

CANTERBURY CL

WINCHESTER DR

WAY

RYDER

DRIVE

The Shropshire P.H.

LANE

Golf Driving Range

WOODSPRINGS GRO

DORCHESTER CLOSE

CALDER GRO

WEYBOURNE WK

LEIGH GRO

Club House

Golf   Course

MARSHBROOK

Muxton Grange Cottages

Millingtons Coppice

6

New Lodge

E   F   G   H

35

A B 24 C D

B4394
STATION
BROOME RD
B4394
P

1 Cross Green

Sports Grnd

2 Wrockwardine Farm

Wrockwardine

Schools

+ EAST VW THE AVENUE

David's Bank

The Dingle

Cemy
WREKIN VW
WREKIN VW

DRUMMERY

Barn Garden Plantation

Sir William's Covert

3 Leaton Grange

BURCOT ROW

Rocky Covert

Leaton

Upper Leaton Farm

Leaton Quarry

Burcot Gorse

4 Overley Cottages

Overley Hall

Burcot

Overley
B5061

LANE

Lea Rock

5 A5

Cluddley

6

A B C D

HADLEY

THE PRINCESS ROYAL
(TELFORD DISTRICT GENERAL)
HOSP.

Comm Centre

Playground

HADLEY PARK INDUSTRIAL ESTATE

Cemy

THE GROVE

Playing Field

School

Leis Cent

HIGH

MANSE

APLEY R/ABOUT

WHITCHURCH DRIVE

Playing Field

Centenary Theatre Rec Grnd

College

Wrekin College

Playing Field

HAYBRIDGE ROUNDABOUT

Hadley

Works

Haybridge

Fire Sta

Recreation Ground

Schools

Bus Sta
Clinic

Pol Sta

New College

Heather Dr

Telford College of Arts & Technology

Telford United F.C.

Swan Hotel

Arts Centre

School

WATLING STREET

Rec Grnd

BENNETTS BANK

Wrekin Youth Centre

KETLEY BROOK ROUNDABOUT

HOLYHEAD RD

HOLYHEAD ROAD

Works

Old Hall Pool

Cricket Grnd

Schools

Rec Grd

Arleston

Toll

Arleston Village

WREKIN RETAIL PARK

Ketley Dingle

Sports Field

M54

Harrison Gdns

MOUNT GILBERT

Arleston Manor

M54 JUNCTION 6
A5223

Golf Course

Arleston Hill

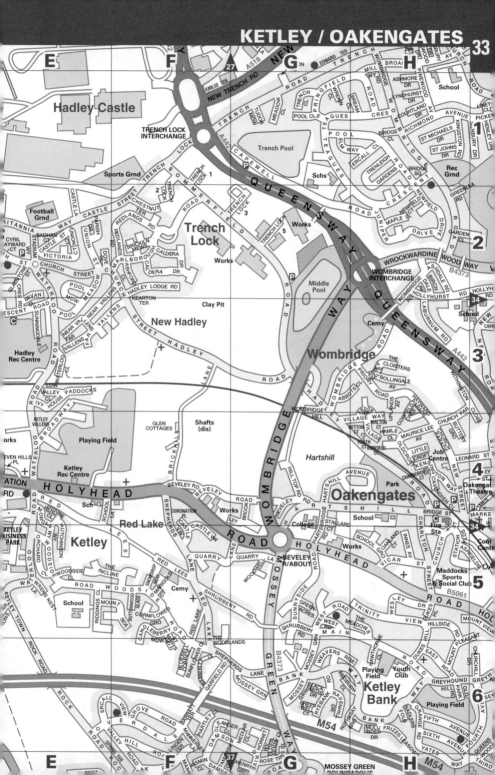

E F G H

New L

1

GRANVILLE

ROAD

GRANVILLE

GRANGE

Ferndale
Farm

NVILLE

P

Granville
Country Park

Cooper's
Coppice

2

ROAD

WOODHOUSE

Dawes
Bower

Woodhouse
Farm

LANE

3

GRANGE

LANE

Watling Street
Grange

4

Crematorium

Reservoir

LANE

KILN BANK
NDABOUT

VXACONA
Roman Settlement
(Site of)

WATLING STREET

ROMAN ROAD

A5

Redhill

Redhill

Sch

SHAFTES-
BURY

MAYFAIR
GRO

WYNDHAM

HOLBOURN
GRO

HIGHGATE DR

LAMBETH

WEST MINSTER WAY

COMBE

COLLIFORD

Medical
Centre

Rec Grnd

Upper
Woodhouse Farm

Woodgreen

5

HIGHGROVE
MDWS

CHANCERY
PK

YORK

ELTHAM
DR

CASTLE

HEREFORD

SOUTH

WELLS
CLOSE

ROAD

WATERLOW
CL

FORSYTHIA
CL

AZALEA
CL

CAMELLIA
DR

FUCHSIA
CL

LLUNA
DR

AVENUE

ELY

FINCHLEY

SALISBURY

LICHFIELD
CL

FARM

ELIA

CHILCOMBE
DR

LILYWALE
CL

KEW
GDNS

WOODHOUSE

The Woodhouse

STOCKFORD

IAN

KESWORTH
DR

WAY

CA

B5060

LANE

WO

Wards Roughs

E F G H

29

39

A   Arlesto **B**lill   C   D

1

Steeraway

Short Wood

Limekiln Lane

Dawley Lane

Dawley Road

Arleston

Lawley Furnaces

Ketley Brook

Silver Birches

2

Limekiln Wood

New Works Lane

School

Glendale

Snedshill Mdws

Lawley

Millman Gro

To Moa Cl

Bartholomew Ln

3

Black Hayes

Birch Coppice

New Works

Church

The Meadows

Highfield

Glendale

Glendale

Playing Field

Bawley Hill

Wellington

Lawley Common R/About

Road

Footbridge

4

Lower Huntington Farm

Dog In The Lane

Club House

Lawley

Wellington Road

Lawley

Horse Comm

5

Huntington

Lyde Brook

Horsehay Village Golf Course

Golf Course

New Row Spring

Spring Village

Spring

Pool View

Horse Po

6

Lydebrook Farm

Simpsons Pool

Simpsons Ln

Farm Mdw

Farm Cl

Club

Foresters Cl

Wellington Road

Bridge

Woodhou

Ind Es

Coal

A   B   40   C   D   A5223

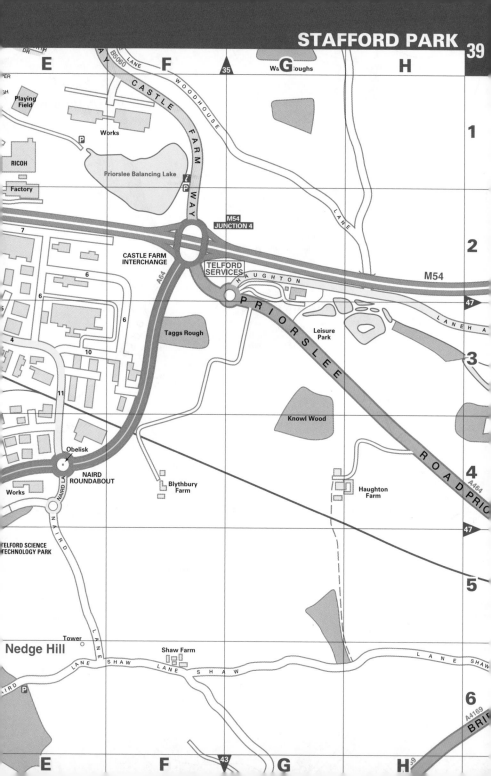

E   F   G   H

Playing
Field

Works

RICOH

P

Factory

Priorslee Balancing Lake

ℹ
P

1

35

Wa G oughs

WOODHOUSE

CASTLE FARM WAY

B5060

LANE

LANE

M54
JUNCTION 4

CASTLE FARM
INTERCHANGE

TELFORD
SERVICES

A464

7

6

6

6

4

10

Taggs Rough

HAUGHTON

PRIORSLEE

Leisure
Park

M54

47

LANE H A

2

3

11

Obelisk

NAIRD
ROUNDABOUT

Blythbury
Farm

Knowl Wood

ROAD PRIC

Haughton
Farm

A464

47

4

Works

NAIRD LA

NAIRD

TELFORD SCIENCE
TECHNOLOGY PARK

5

Tower

Nedge Hill

LANE

P

NAIRD

SHAW LANE

Shaw Farm

SHAW

LANE

LANE SHAW

A4169

BRI

6

E   F   G   H

43

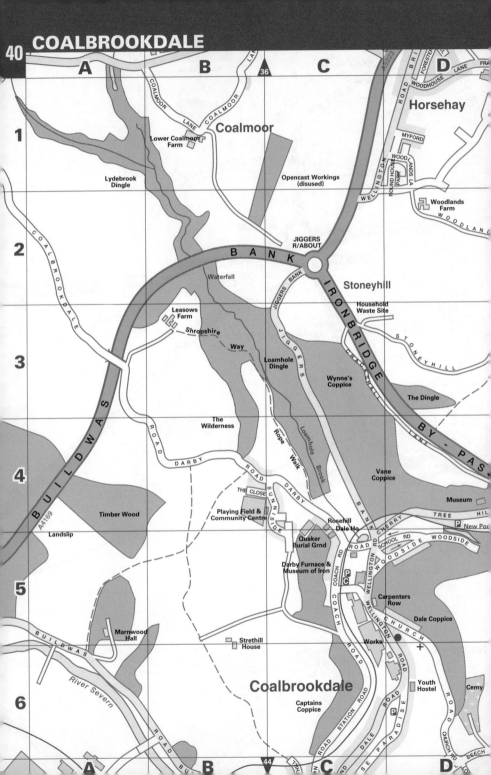

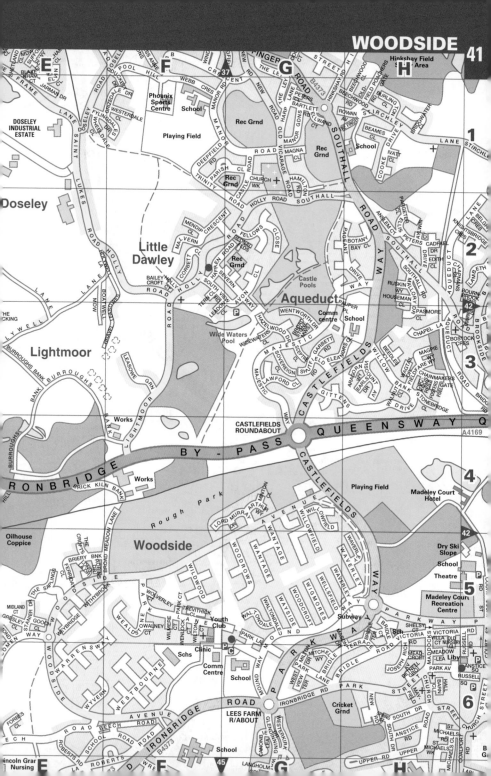

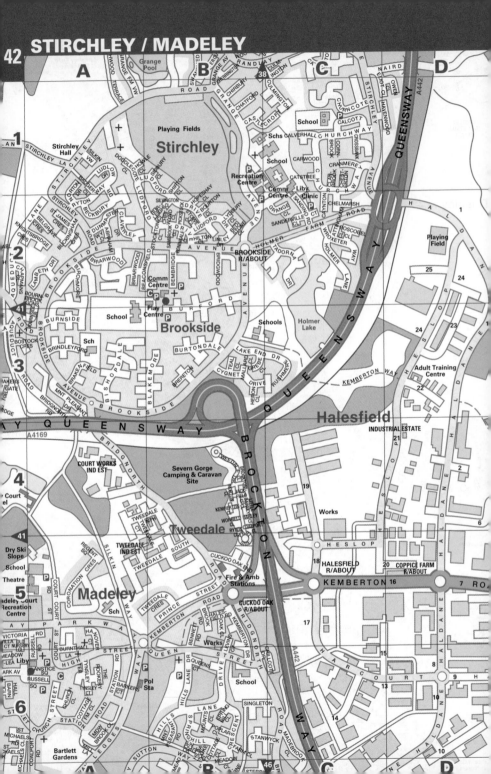

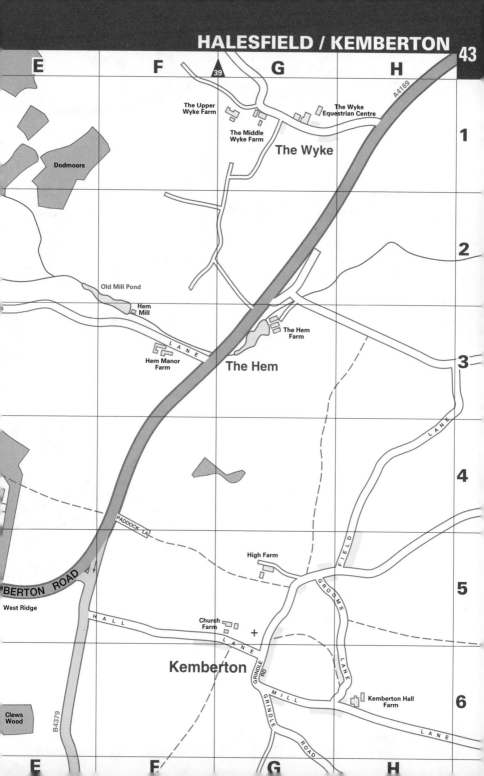

E   F   39   G   H

The Upper Wyke Farm

The Wyke Equestrian Centre

The Middle Wyke Farm

The Wyke

A4169

1

Dodmoors

2

Old Mill Pond

Hem Mill

The Hem Farm

LANE

Hem Manor Farm

The Hem

3

LANE

4

PADDOCK LA

High Farm

FIELD

5

BERTON ROAD

West Ridge

GROOMS

HALL

LANE

LANE

Church Farm

+

Kemberton

GRINDLE RD

MILL

Kemberton Hall Farm

LANE

Clews Wood

B4379

GRINDLE ROAD

LANE

E   F   G   H

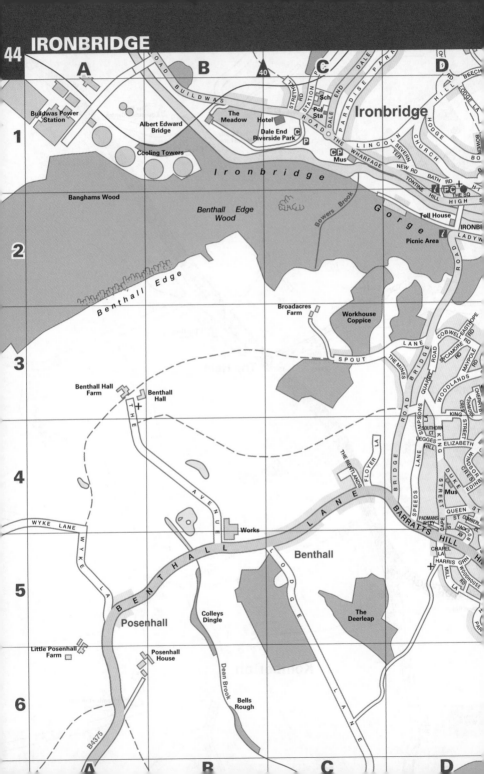

A **B** **40** **C** **D**

Buildwas Power Station

Albert Edward Bridge

Cooling Towers

The Meadow

Hotel

Dale End Riverside Park

Sch

Pol Sta

Ironbridge

BUILDWAS ROAD

STRETTON RD

STATION RD

DALE END

PARADISE

THE PARA

DALE

HILL

HODGE

CHURCH RD

BEECH

LODGE LA

BOWER

1

I r o n b r i d g e

Banghams Wood

Benthall Edge Wood

Bowers Brook

CP Mus

WHARFAGE

SEVERN TER

NEW RD

LINCOLN

BATH RD

TONTINE HILL

PC THE SQ HIGH

Toll House

IRONB

2

G o r g e

Picnic Area

LADYW

ROAD

B e n t h a l l   E d g e

Broadacres Farm

Workhouse Coppice

SPOUT

THE MINES

LANE

COBWELL RD

EASTHOPE RD

QUARRY ROAD

BRIDGE ROAD

SYCAMORE RD

MAYPOLE RD

WOODLANDS

CHERRERD

3

Benthall Hall Farm

Benthall Hall

THE

SIMPSONS LA

SOUTHORN CT

LEGGES HILL

KING STREET

CREST

ASHMORE CREST

KING

ELIZABETH

WINDSOR CRES

EDINB

Benthall Hall

AVENUE

THE BENTLANDS

FLOYER LA

BRIDGE ROAD

SPEEDS LANE

CAPE ST

DUKE STREET

Mus

QUEEN ST

CUMBERL

4

WYKE LANE

WYKE LA

Works

BENTHALL LANE

Benthall

LODGE LANE

BARRATS HILL

PADMANS ALLEY

JACKSON

AV

CHAPEL LA

HARRIS GRN

MILL LA

WOODHOUSE RD

PAR

5

Posenhall

Colleys Dingle

The Deerleap

Little Posenhall Farm

Posenhall House

Dean Brook

Bells Rough

B4375

6

A **B** **C** **D**

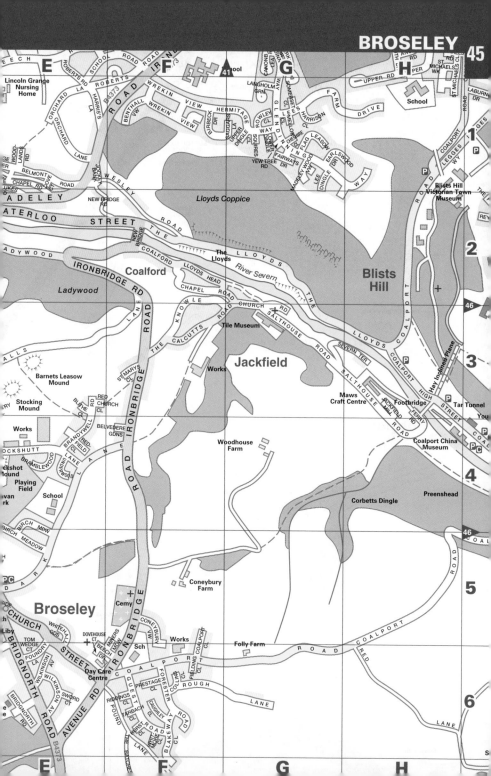

A map page of Coalport, Sutton Hill and surrounding area.

Grid references A, B, C, D (top and bottom) and 1–6 (sides).

Bartlett Gardens

ST MIC
LABURNUM DR

COALPORT RD
LEGGES WY
LEGGES

P

SUTTON WAY
SUMMERHILL

Sutton Hill
P
CL
Clinic
Liby
Comm Centre
School

SOUTHGATE
SOUTHGATE
SMALLWOOD
SUTTON
DRIVE

REYNARDS MDW
THE FOXES COPPICE
REYNARDS

MIMOSA WAY
VERBENA WAY
THE HAY
PUNTA VERDE DR
TROON COURT
CARNOUSTIE
GLENEAGLES CL
GREAT

SELBOURNE CL
SHAWFIELD CL
STONEDALE

SUNNYMEAD
MEADOW

STANWYOK
CRE FARMCL
CARLINE
STEBBINGS

SPRING MDW
SPRNG MDW
SPRNG

BRIDGNORTH RD
SOLWAY
WAY
BD SE
KIRK

SANDCROFT

SOUTHFIELD
SCOTT DR
SPURN WAY
SWINBUR
SHAKESPEARE WY
SHELLEY
SPENCER DR
SHERIDAN WY

STOKESAY FORE
STOKESAY
STOKESAY GRN
STOKESAY
WAY
STRETTON CL
STIRLING DR

BROCKTON R/ABOUT
A442

SUTTON HILL R/ABOUT
Playing Field

Sutton Wood

HALDANE
BRIDGNORTH
ROAD

44
C

Brockton Court

45
Inclined Plane

Telford Hotel Golf & Country Club

Great Hay Golf Course

Monarchs Way

Sutton Hill Farm
Sutton Hill House

Brickkiln Coppice

Monarchs Way

Tar Tunnel
Youth Hostel
P
Coalport
RIVERSIDE
P C
COALPORT

t China eum

HIGH STREET

Sutton Wood Farm

4

Coalport Bridge

enshead

45
COALPORT ROAD

Sweyney Cliff

The Wilds

Sweyney Cliff House

Sutton Wood

River Seven

Caravan Site

ROAD

5

Rowton House

Sewage Works

6
LANE

Tarbatch Dingle

Swinbatch

A   B   C   D

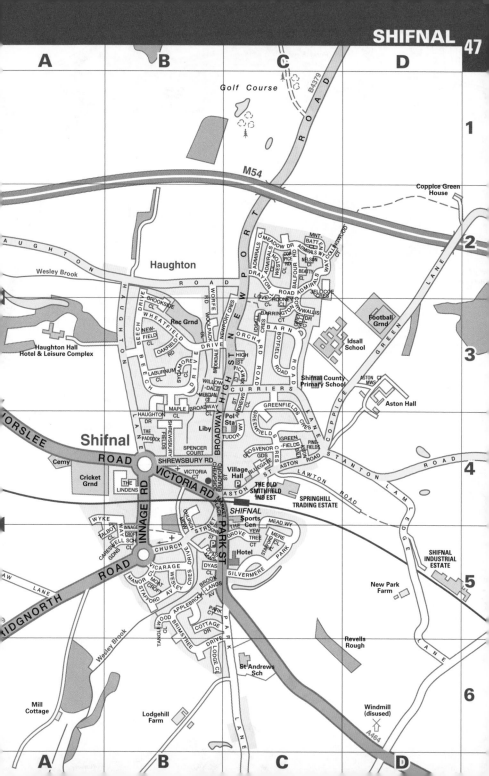

Golf Course

B4379

M54

Coppice Green House

1

2

Wesley Brook

Haughton

HAUGHTON

Haughton Hall Hotel & Leisure Complex

Rec Grnd

BROOKSIDE

WHEATFIELD

BEECH DRIVE

NEW-FIELD CL

OAKFIELD RD

LABURNUM CL

SYCAMORE RD

MAPLE

HAUGHTON DR

THE PADDOCK

SHREWSBURY FIELDS

WORFE RD

WOOLPACK CRES

BROOKDALE RD

WILLOW-DALE

MERCIAN CT

BROADWAY

NEWPORT ROAD

DRAYTON ROAD

MEADOW DR

ADMIRALS CL

WEST

COPPICE RD

BALFOUR

NELSON CT

BEATTY

LOVE

RODNEY CL

BARRINGTON CT

IDSALL CRES

HIGH ST PL

ORCHARD ROAD

BARN

BOTFIELD ROAD

CURRIERS LANE

HIGH STREET

ST ANDREWS CT

ST

GREENFIELDS

GREENFIELDS CRES

MNT-BATTEN

ADMIRALS WY

COLLINGWOOD WAY

JELLICOE CRES

ADMIRALS

CORNWALLIS

GREEN DR

CL

Football Grnd

Idsall School

Shifnal County Primary School

ASTON CT MWS

Aston Hall

COPPICE

GREEN LANE

STANTON LANE

3

Shifnal

TORSLEE

Cemy

ROAD

Cricket Grnd

THE LINDENS

SHREWSBURY RD

VICTORIA CT

Liby

SPENCER COURT

VICTORIA RD

INNAGE RD

CROSSWELL CEAPSIDE

MARKET PLACE

ASTON

BROADWAY

Pol Sta

TUDOR WY

GROSVENOR GDS

BLUEGATE

ST

GREEN-FIELDS

PINE FIELDS

GROSVENOR CRES

ASTON ROAD

LAWTON ROAD

STANTON LANE

ROAD

LEDGE

ROAD

4

Village Hall

THE OLD SMITHFIELD IND EST

SPRINGHILL TRADING ESTATE

SHIFNAL INDUSTRIAL ESTATE

5

WYKE LANE

TALBOT CL

INNAGE CROFT

CARESWELL SCH

GDNS

CHURCH DRIVE

CHURCH STREET

ST MARYS

VICARAGE

MANOR STAFFORD

MOAT CROFT

AV

WESLEY CRES

DYAS CL

BROOK

LLANDS AV

PARK ST

SHIFNAL

GROVE

Sports Gen

YEW TREE CT

MEAD WY

STAFFORD CL

MERE CL

PARK

SILVERMERE

Hotel

BRIDGNORTH ROAD

INNAGE ROAD

TANGLEWOOD

APPLEBROOK DR

BRIMSTREE

COTTAGE DR

PARK CT

LODGE CT

PARK DRIVE

PARK

New Park Farm

Revells Rough

SHIFNAL INDUSTRIAL ESTATE

LANE

5

St Andrews Sch

6

Mill Cottage

Wesley Brook

LANE

Lodgehill Farm

Windmill (disused)

A464

A   B   C   D

A B C D

Pond Bay

M54

N
E
A
C
H
L
E
Y

Tong Lodge

Orchard Covert

Neachley Bridge

1

Castle Wood

M54 JUNCTION 3

NEWPORT

New Build Farm

A41

Neachley Hall

Birch Wood

Neach Hill

Kilsall Hall

Cosford

Neachley House

Ruckleywood Farm

Neachley Pool

2

Kilsall Farm

LANE

L
O
N
G

L
A
N
E

N
E
A
C
H
L
E
Y

L
A
N
E

LEUCHERS LANE

LEUCHERS LANE

LEOMINGTON

FLEMING

MARTLESHAM

RADFORD

AVENUE

CHESHIRE LINES

BATH

CONINGSBY

WASHAM

WADDINGTON

LEEMING

R.A.F
COSFORD

R
O
A
D

K
I
N
L
O
S
S

W
A
Y

ROAD

LANE

3

ROAD

THE OVAL SWIN DERBY CL

Worfe

LYSANDER

AVENUE

HUDSON RD

MAGISTER RD

ISTBURE

AVENUE

TRO W BRIDGE RD

WHIT CHURCH

TR EN CHARD RD

Aerospace Museum

COSFORD

Indoor Athletics Centre

Sports Stadium

Sports Ground

WORCESTER

ROAD

4

B O R S A

The Royal Air Force Museum

COSFORD AIRFIELD

Chappel House Farm

5

Hillbank Wood

Cosford Pool

Pool Covert

Cosford Grange Farm

Sewage Works

WORCESTER

OLD

ROAD

H O L Y H E A D

A464

Piggeries

Bowling Green House

LANE

GREEN

6

ROAD

A464

Sewage Works

LA KENNEL LANE

BOWLING

Nursery

A B C D

E   F   G   H

1

Tong Park
Farm

Monarchs Way

Parkhorn
Rough

Shackerley
Farm

M54

OLD SHACKERLEY LANE

SHACKERLEY LANE

Shackerley

2

R.A.F STATION
COSFORD

Shackerley
Hall

CIRCULAR ROAD   HALIFAX RD
WESTERN   CASTER   BLENHEIM CRES
BOURN   STIRLING RD   LANCASTER CL
ARCHIV...   WELLINGTON   DENIS...
ABINGDON   SYDNAL LA
RD   LANE

MILL   LANE

SHACKERLEY LANE

Innage

Lower Wood
Farm

Caravan
Park

DONINGTON   LANE

3

LANE

CORDY

Donington
House

DONINGTON

New
Plantation

LANE

4

NEWPORT   RD
VICTOR   ST VINCENT

ALBRIGHTON   ROAD

SHACKERLEY   LANE

Garden
Centre
Nursery

SANDY

Blue
House

BLUE   HOUSE   LANE

Albrighton
Trust

Moat

Humphreston
Hall

Donington

Football
Grnd
Fire
Sta

WORTHINGTON DR
BLOCK
MILLS
GRANGE
PARK   ROAD
RECTORY
WHITE LADIES

Albrighton

St Cuthberts
Well

Albrighton
Pool

5

HARRIOTTS HAYES   RD

ALBRIGHTON

BY - PASS

6

ST CUTHBERTS CRES
GREEN
BOWLING   ROAD
TALBOT
BELA   WARE
DELAWARE   AVENUE
CHURCH   ROAD
OLD HALL
PITCHFORD   RD
BISHTON   RD
CROSS
NEWHOUSE
GARRIDGE   CL
BISHTON

Club

GRANGE RD
GRANGE
ROAD
ABNEY
CHARLES
MAYFIELD RD
LYNCROFT
ALBERT RD
WHISTON
SHELDON
CT
MANOR
RICHARDSON ROAD
WOLVER...
CT
THE
FISH
LANES

Club

ST MARYS GLEBE
BREDON
THE
BUSHFIELD
BARRINGTON
RD
BUSH
Liby

P

Pol
Sta

STATION   ROAD
WINDSOR   ROAD
CEDAR   RD
FAIR   LAWN
WESTON   ROD
MEADOW   ROAD
FAIR LAWN
CT

TELFORD   AV
BARCLAY   AV
BRINDLEY   ROAD
COTSWOLD   CL
EASTER   CL
REDFARM
SHAW

BROOKLANDS
RD
Road

ALBRIGHTON

St Marys
Primary
School

KINGSWOOD   ROAD
BEAMISH   LANE

Albrighton
Hall

Albrighton County
Schools

E   F   G   H

Church Stretton

Grid references:
- 1, 2, 3, 4
- A, B, C, D, E, F

Labels on map:
- Helmeth Hill
- Battle Field
- Houghs Coppice
- Caradoc Coppice
- New House Farm
- High Leyes
- BY-PASS
- A49
- STRETTON
- LANE
- Castle Hill
- Woodnall
- All Stretton
- Row Castle
- B4370
- HILL
- ROAD
- THE
- STARR LANE
- HEIGHWAYS LA
- FARM
- Synalds Farm
- Camping & Caravan Site
- Springbank Farm
- Church Stretton
- Church Stretton Sch
- Well Well Well Water Ltd
- Sports Ground
- Swimming Pool
- Primary School
- THE PADDOCK
- BODBURY
- Nover's Hill
- Enclosure
- YELD BANK
- LONGMYND
- BODBURY CT
- ASHBROOK CRES
- CHATWELL
- CHURCHILL
- CL
- ASH-BROOK CT
- KENNEDY CL
- SANDF
- LUTW-YCHE CL
- Brooksbury Rec Grnd
- Russels Mdw (Playing Field)
- ESSEX
- ASCOT CL
- WINDSOR
- Fire Sta
- Works
- Park
- NORTH STREET
- HELMETH CMWS
- OAKS DR
- ALI
- LING
- Cwmdale Farm
- BURROW
- RABBIT HILL
- MADEIRA
- WALK
- STANYELD RD
- SAINTS RD
- REV
- Club House
- Stanyeld
- VALLEY
- Ashbrook
- MILL
- LONGHILLS
- CARDING
- RECTORY GDNS
- Old Rectory Wood
- ROAD
- Hall
- Golf Course
- Park Coppice
- Bodbury Ring
- Bodbury Hill
- Carding
- Mill Valley
- Devil's Mouth
- Burway Hill
- BURWAY
- Reservoir
- Haddon Hill
- Devilsmouth Hollow
- Pool Hollow
- Cross Dyke
- Town Brook
- Townbrook Valley

A   B   C   D

1

2

3

4

5

6

Hoards Park

pit tion

Pond Bay

Tasley

Water Tower

Church Farm

The Hook Dingle

Cantern

Brook

Cantreyn

Cantern Bank

Cantern Farm

BROSELEY

Golf Driving Range

DUNVAL RD
DUNVAL DR
FOSTER RD
DR WHITMORE
PRINCESS
QUEENSWAY
DUCHESS
CANTREYN
GREENFIELDS
DINGLE VIEW
GREENFIELDS CRES
GREENFIELDS DR
GREENFIELDS CT

St Leonards C of E Junior Sch

STANL LANE IND ES

STANLEY

Racecourse Farm

Auction Rooms

BRIDGNORTH

WENLOCK

A458

The Leasowes

MARCH-WOOD
BEACONSFIELD
COPPERFIELD
ABBEYFIELD
FAIRFIELD
HOOK ROAD
COTTAGE DR
BEECH
VICTORIA
LINKEY RD
ROAD
FARM

WREKIN
CLEE
MWRIGHTON
SYDNEY DR
TOWERS CL
RACECOURSE
LEASOWES CL
LANE

ASH
ROAD GDNS
OAK
COTTAGE WAY

The Woodberry P.H

WOODBERRY
WOODBERRY CL

ELIZABETH
SYDNEY
AV

The Hookfield
ORCHARD

Bridgnorth Infants Sch

Innage Centre

Andrew Evans Ho

Amo Fire Sta
Sta

Innage Grange

St Johns R.C Primary Sch

Bridgno Endow Sch

Spor Fiel

INNAGE

RICHMOND GDNS

INNAGE

ROAD

NORTH

Leisu Cen

Crown Meadows (Playing Field)

High Town

BRIDGNORTH Cricket Grnd

BRIDGNORTH HOSPITAL

CLIFF

MOAT

Bowling green

North Gate Museum

CLAREMONT

CRICKET ROAD

WESTGATE

MDW

Supermarket

WHITBURN ST

THREE ASHES
FARMLANDS RD
HIGHFIELDS

PORTMANS WY

RIDLEY
TINING
MAUDLINS
LUDLOW HEIGHTS

HARLEY
ASHCROFT
CL

WHEATLANDS
WHEATLANDS RISE
WESTLAND DR

WESTLAND
HUNTSMANS
LANE

Pol Sta

Bridgnorth D.C Offices

Pauls Pool

WESTGATE DRIVE

SALOP ROAD

PAULBROO RD

CONDUIT LA

AVON DALE CL
ROSEHILL DRIVE

VALLEY SQUIRREL CT
CLOSE

Central Cl
Shopping Arcade

ST MARYS
LISTLEY ST
ST MARYS CT

HIGH ST

RAILWAY ST

POUND ST

WELLS

HOLL BUSH

Poste Gate

Liby

WEST CASTLE RD

NEW RO

LUDLOW ROAD

Round Thorn

STRETTON
CONDUIT
RAMSON
CASTLEFIELDS

HIGH-LANDS RD

HIGHLANDS

MANOR
ROAD

DELGHTONS
MORGAN
SPRINGS
OLDBURY

WELLS ROAD

WELLS CLOSE

THE HAWTHORNS

HILLY BK
OLDBURY TER
SPARROW CT

Playing Fields

Tennis Courts

Oldbury Wells School

BRIDGNORTH (Severn Valley Railway)

Hundred House Farm

Schools

CAPTAINS RD
MEADOW CL

Swimming Pool

Motte & Bailey

OLDBURY

FELLS ORCHARD

Bridgnorth

BY - PASS ROAD

Panpudding Hill

rook e

LUDLOW ROAD

B4364

Cross Houses

Thornton Farm

Henley Lodge

MANOR FARM LANE

Manor Court

Oldbury

OLDBURY
B4363

OLD MILL LANE

Dani Brid

B4473

E | F | G | H

1

2

3

4

5

6

Club House

The Batch

Burcote Villa

Woodside

Fenn Gate

RIVER SEVERN

ROAD

A442

Bridgnorth Golf Course

Fort Pendlestone

Pendlestone Rock

High Rock Coppice

Jacobs Ladder

High Rock

BATCH LANE

A454

Swancote Cottages

The Hobbins

Sports Ground

Tippings Cross Coppice

Cemetery

B4363

ROAD

Caves

The Hermitage

Hermitage Farm

Football Grnd

Bridgnorth Rowing Club

Low Town

Queens Parlor

Reservoir (covered)

Hermitage Hill Coppice

BRIDGE ST

The Bylet

School

ELMHURST

PINEWAY

MILL STREET

TELFORD

WOLVERHAMPTON ROAD

HERMITAGE

The Mall

INDUSTRIAL ESTATE

To STANMORE INDUSTRIAL ESTATE

The Grove

A458

College of Further Education

BY - PASS

STOURBRIDGE

ROAD

A458 ROAD

Sports Ground

Warehouse

Gatacrehill Plantation

Essex Fall

The Riverside Caravan Park

BRIDGNORTH

KIDDERMINSTER

BRIDGNORTH LITHO Works

Depot

WORCESTER

Maze

Spring Valley Farm

Gallows Field

Danesford

Football Grnd Sports Ground

Spring Valley

ROAD

A442

Daniels Mill

E | F | G | H

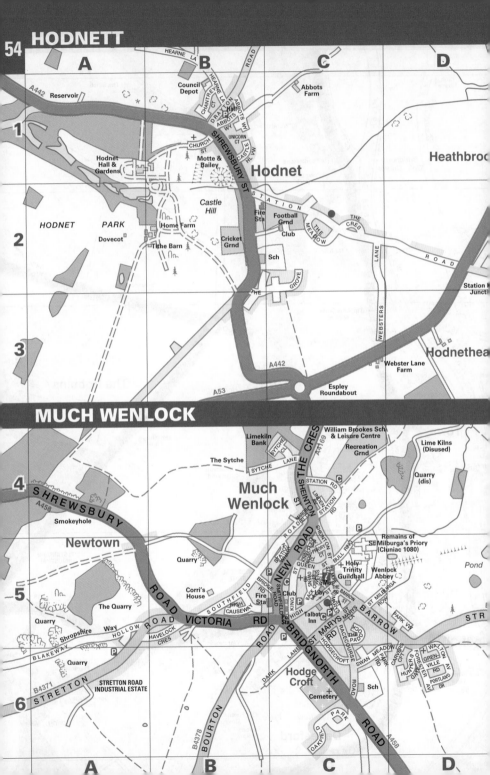